BUTTERFLIES

Exploring the Life Cycle

Written by Dr. Shirley Raines

Photography by Curt Hart

To Kendra,
Shirley Raines

Discover butterflies with photos, fun facts, and verse

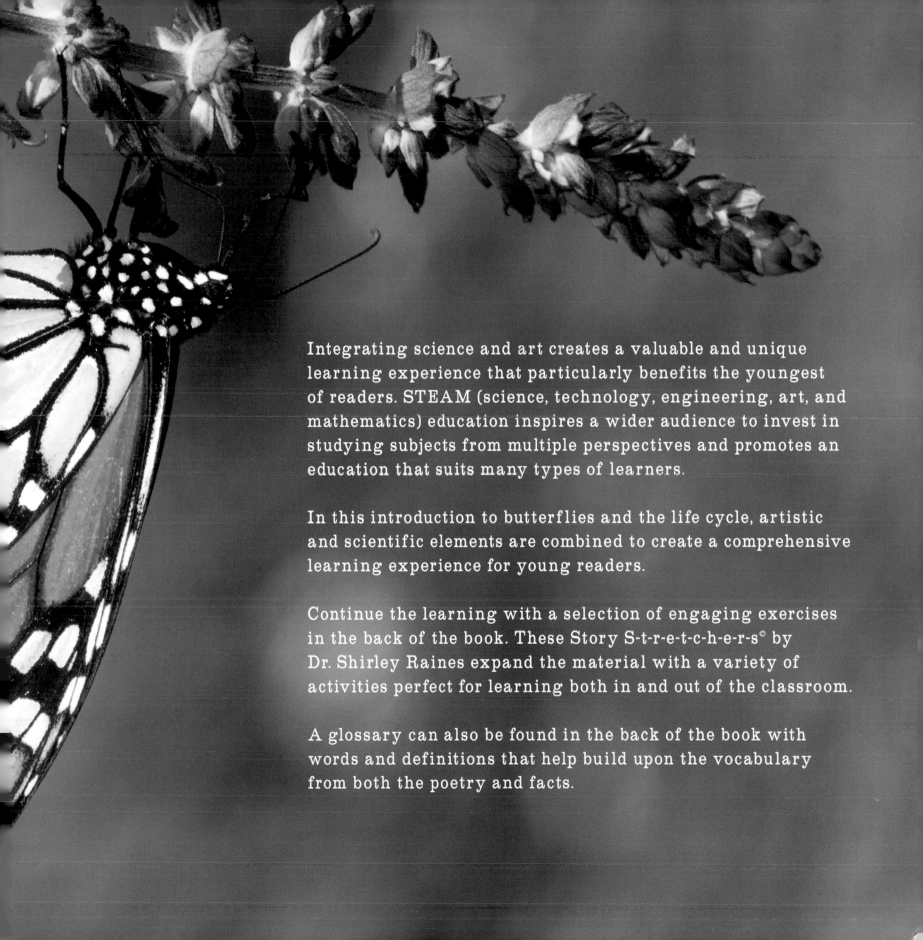

Integrating science and art creates a valuable and unique learning experience that particularly benefits the youngest of readers. STEAM (science, technology, engineering, art, and mathematics) education inspires a wider audience to invest in studying subjects from multiple perspectives and promotes an education that suits many types of learners.

In this introduction to butterflies and the life cycle, artistic and scientific elements are combined to create a comprehensive learning experience for young readers.

Continue the learning with a selection of engaging exercises in the back of the book. These Story S-t-r-e-t-c-h-e-r-s© by Dr. Shirley Raines expand the material with a variety of activities perfect for learning both in and out of the classroom.

A glossary can also be found in the back of the book with words and definitions that help build upon the vocabulary from both the poetry and facts.

What Will I Grow Up to Be?

What will I grow up to be?
Who can guess by looking at me?

I'm just a tiny little egg,
but someday I'll have six legs.

I'm changing into a wiggler.
I'll tickle you into a giggler.

A caterpillar with hairy spikes
to hold onto leaves that I like.

What will I grow up to be?
Who can guess by looking at me?

Changing again, starting at my head.
I'm wrapping myself up in a bed.

In this bed hanging by a thread,
I am a chrysalis it is said.

Inside I change for my surprise.
A delight for your lovely eyes.

When I come out, ever so slow,
I dry my wings in the sun's glow.

What will I grow up to be?
Who can guess by looking at me?

I am a monarch butterfly.
I am a beauty in the sky.

Butterfly Makeover

To become the beautiful butterfly we love, this tiny creature goes through big changes—four big changes, to be exact. This is called the life cycle. First, a female butterfly must lay an egg on a host plant. The egg is the first stage. This egg then hatches into a caterpillar or larva, which is the second stage. That caterpillar then spends time eating until it is ready for the third stage called the pupa stage. This is when the caterpillar forms a chrysalis. And finally, the fourth stage comes when a butterfly emerges!

For most butterflies, the pupa stage lasts between 8 and 15 days.

A butterfly's vibrant colors can be seen through the chrysalis right before they emerge.

Since the chrysalis can't move, it uses camouflage to hide from predators.

Meta-Meta-Metamorphosis

How change happens, who can say?
I want to see it near.
Meta-meta-metamorphosis right here.

Find the eggs on a leaf.
See the caterpillar growing fat.
Watch the chrysalis spinning round.

Ohh! Ahh! Wow!
The butterfly is here.
The mystery revealed.

Meta-meta-metamorphosis,
a change in shape and form.
It's how the butterfly is born.

Presto Change-O!

Butterflies undergo one of the most incredible transformations of any animal in the world. The most dramatic moment of their impressive makeover comes during the pupa stage. The pupa stage can last a few days or a few months, depending on the butterfly. In this stage, fluid inside the chrysalis helps to break down the caterpillar's body and build the butterfly's body. Once the butterfly is ready it will emerge, completing the pupa stage.

Butterflies are found on all of the continents except Antarctica.

Butterflies actually have four wings, not just two. They have two forewings in the front and two hind wings in the back.

Butterflies have an exoskeleton around their body to protect them.

Larva or Caterpillar

I am a larva, that's my name,
but caterpillar is the same.
Straight from the egg I climb
to munch green leaves until it's time.

I grow so fast and I shed my skin,
molting out of my skin so thin.
Not enough leaves for lunch,
need more to crunch, crunch, crunch.

Eating, eating is my game,
puffed up larva is my name.
Crawling on each branch and leaf.
Gobbling up greens, no time to sleep.

Stop! What can it be?
I'm wrapping up. I'm covering me.

Instars of the Show

Much like a butterfly goes through stages, the caterpillar goes through stages of its own. These stages are called instars. As a caterpillar eats, it begins to grow out of its skin. This is called molting. When the caterpillar molts, it sheds its old skin and replaces it with a new skin. Every time a caterpillar molts, it begins a new instar. Caterpillars usually go through about five instars before finally being able to move on to the pupa stage.

Head

Thorax

Legs

Prolegs

Abdomen

The caterpillar or larva stage is usually the longest life stage.

Caterpillar No More

I was a caterpillar who couldn't soar.
But I'm a caterpillar no more.

Caterpillars gobble up their food.
Crunching and munching is so rude.

Butterflies flit and fly,
sipping nectar from flowers up high.

Caterpillars crawl so slow,
nibbling everything as they go.

Butterflies drink and sip
through their straw—their sipping lip.

Caterpillars stay where they're born.
Some look like they have a tiny horn.

Butterflies travel near and far.
Some think they are guided by a star.

I'm a caterpillar no more.
Now I can fly. Now I can soar.

Hungry, Hungry Caterpillars

A caterpillar has one job once it leaves its egg, and it is to eat, eat, eat! Caterpillars need to grow so they can complete their metamorphosis. And they need a lot of food in order to grow! Caterpillars are pretty picky eaters and tend to only like the leaves of their host plant, or the plant where they hatched, but once they find a snack they like, they will munch away! If enough caterpillars are eating together, you can hear crunching sounds as they take their tiny bites.

Caterpillars can consume 3 times their body weight daily during this life stage.

Even though it looks like there are many more, a caterpillar only has 6 true legs. The other "legs" you see are false legs called prolegs.

A caterpillar's very first meal is its own eggshell!

Butterfly, You Are Free

. . . .

When the caterpillar squirms from the egg,
she wants to be free.
When the chrysalis is broken by a tiny leg,
he wants to be free.
When the butterfly flits and flies,
she wants to be free.
When the butterfly soars high,
he wants to be free.
Wait, butterfly, I want to say goodbye.
Now, butterfly, you are free.

Breaking Free

Once a butterfly completes the third life stage and emerges from the chrysalis, it needs time to adjust before it can begin flying. Butterflies need to wait for each wing to dry in the sun and for blood to fill each tiny vein before they can be used. This process usually takes about 30 minutes and leaves the butterfly vulnerable to predators. However, once the process is complete, the butterfly can finally take flight!

Painted lady butterflies, like this one, drink flower nectar but some butterflies will also drink from overripe fruit.

Butterflies need the warmth of the sun in order to fly.

A butterfly's wings move in a figure eight motion when they fly.

6, 4, 2, 1

....

6, 4, 2, 1
6 legs, 4 wings, 2 antennae, and one of other things.
1 body in 2 parts, the thorax and the abdomen.
Where's the heart?
1 large eye with many views.
1 sipping tongue, that's the news.
4 wings, a beautiful sight.
Hind wings, forewings, flying to the sun.
Butterfly shape.
6, 4, 2, 1

Sizing Butterflies Up

Butterflies come in all shapes and sizes. Some butterflies can be as small as less than an inch (less than 2.54 centimeters) from wing to wing, while others can be up to 12 inches (30.4 centimeters) long! The largest butterfly in the United States is the giant swallowtail measuring about 5.5 inches (13.9 centimeters), while the smallest butterfly is the western pygmy blue butterfly measuring about half an inch (1.2 centimeters) long.

Antennae

Proboscis

Thorax

Compound Eye

Forewing

Hind Wing

Abdomen

Butterflies are nearsighted and can only see up to 12 feet (3.6 meters) away.

Butterfly Wings

Butterfly wings are colorful things.
Some are yellow.
Some are brown.
Some are the color of the ground.

Speckles and flecks of dusty gold,
much too fragile to hold.

Butterfly wings are beautiful things.
See the blue ones and azure too.
Jewel colors in green, red, and blue.
Colors in every hue.

Clearly Colorful

Butterfly wings are some of the most beautiful and delicate things in the whole world. Depending on the type of butterfly, they can be brightly colored or even covered in spots, but did you know that a butterfly's wings are made of a thin layer of protein called chitin? This layer of protein is so thin that you can actually see right through it! The beautiful colors you see are really thousands of tiny scales that cover the chitin and reflect light, giving the butterfly such beautiful wings!

Most butterflies are only active during the day; very few ever come out at night.

Adult gulf fritillary butterflies, like this one, are known for their quick and erratic movements when they fly.

Butterflies use their antennae to keep their balance and to smell food and other butterflies!

Butterfly Big Words

Metamorphosis,
Chrysalis,
Proboscis.
Big, big words for tiny, tiny butterflies.

Metamorphosis,
Chrysalis,
Proboscis.
So many butterfly big words that rhyme.

Metamorphosis.
Butterfly transformer.
Chrysalis.
Safe space former.
Proboscis.
A tongue like a straw absorber.
Big, big words for tiny, tiny butterflies.

Super Sippers

When a butterfly breaks free from its chrysalis, it has gone through a lot of changes! One of the most significant changes has to do with their diet. As a caterpillar, it was important to eat leafy plants nonstop, but once a caterpillar becomes a butterfly, they can't munch on plants anymore. Instead of a mouth, they have a proboscis, which is what they use to drink nectar. This proboscis works like a straw and allows the butterfly to sip directly from a flower or fruit. When the butterfly is finished drinking its meal, it curls its proboscis under its chin until it's needed again.

Many butterflies have nicknames; for example, the wings of this butterfly resemble rice paper, which is why it is sometimes called a rice paper butterfly.

Female butterflies tend to live longer than male butterflies.

The fastest butterfly in the world can fly up to 12 miles per hour (19.3 kilometers per hour).

Here We Go Round the Butterfly Bush

Here we go 'round the butterfly bush,
the butterfly bush,
the butterfly bush.
Here we go 'round the butterfly bush
so early in the morning.

More butterflies on the butterfly bush,
the butterfly bush,
the butterfly bush.
More butterflies on the butterfly bush
to drink from pretty flowers.

No dancing 'round the butterfly bush,
the butterfly bush,
the butterfly bush.
No dancing 'round the butterfly bush.
Stop! Don't make a sound!

Shh! Hush! Don't make a sound
while the butterflies are around.
Be still as you can be.
And it could happen, just maybe,
a butterfly will land on me.

Feet Buds?

Butterflies don't have taste buds in their mouth like we do. Instead, they have taste receptors on their feet! These receptors help butterflies find food and find their host plant so that they can lay their eggs. In order to know which plant they have landed on or what they are about to munch on, they will stomp their feet to release the juices in the leaves or to taste the food they are about to consume.

One of the main differences between a moth and a butterfly is how they rest. Butterflies typically keep their wings closed, while moths rest with them open.

Some butterflies only use 4 of their 6 legs. The other 2 legs just rest against their body.

Female butterflies are typically bigger than male butterflies.

Swallowtails

Five kinds of swallowtails I see.
Pointy tails, please fly by me.

Tiger swallowtails are easy finds,
flying near trees and flowers.
Yellow wings with black lines,
lovely looking after little showers.

Black swallowtail butterflies
visit the same place.
All with white spots in a line
and tiny blue spots that shine.

Giant swallowtails are black.
Sipping on citrus is their snack.
Black wings with white spots.
No, those are yellow dots!

Is pipevine swallowtail the same?
How did you get your pipevine name?
Dark, dark shine with iridescent blue
and you lay red eggs, that's a clue!

Zebra swallowtail like your stripes,
flashing black and white types.
Zebra swallowtail, where do you dine
when pawpaw plants are hard to find?

Five kinds of swallowtails I see.
Pointy tails, please fly by me.

Save the Butterflies

Butterflies are such beautiful creatures that many people enjoy collecting them, however, this has played a small role in placing some butterflies on the endangered species list. Not only are humans interfering by taking butterflies from their homes, they have also taken away some of their habitats, leaving a few species on the verge of extinction. There are many organizations and people who are helping the butterflies by creating butterfly gardens, where butterflies can live safely, or planting host plants, where they can lay their eggs.

Butterflies, much like bees, help plants and trees continue to grow by spreading pollen around while they feed on nectar.

Giant swallowtail butterflies, like this one, are the only butterflies that use a citrus tree as their host plant.

There are more than 750 butterfly species in the United States!

Leaving Day

· ·

It is leaving day.
I'm finding my way.

Navigation without a map.
Migration, avoiding the traps.

Wake up, it's flying day!
Do you rest along the way?

Stop, please, at my little garden.
A sip of nectar for you to go farther.

So sad, it's leaving day.
I hope the butterflies find their way.

Masters of Migration

Monarch butterflies migrate south during the winter each year in search of food and warmer weather. Monarchs will travel during the day, then huddle together, or roost, at night to stay warm. Monarchs can travel up to 100 miles (160.9 kilometers) a day and it typically takes them 2 months to make it to their destination!

Some butterflies, like the monarch butterfly, are poisonous, so predators have learned to recognize their bright wings and stay away!

A group of butterflies is sometimes called a flutter.

Female monarchs have thicker veins in their wings than males.

I Spy

I spy with my little eye
six eyes staring back at me.
Is that how the buckeye butterfly
can see?

I spy with my little eye
six eyes on wings.
Do you really see things
through your wings?

I spy with my little eye
wings you fold out.
Decorated things
ready to fly about.

I spy with my little eye
your big eye atop your head,
not on the wing you use to fly.
I may have been misled!

Hiding in Plain Sight

Butterflies are usually an appetizing meal for predators, such as birds, wasps, and snakes, but many butterflies have developed tricks to avoid being eaten. Most butterflies use some form of camouflage. They use their wings to help them hide among plants or leaves. Others choose to flaunt their bright colors to show predators that they are poisonous. And there are even some super sneaky butterflies that copy their colorful cousin's wing coloring and pretend to be poisonous just to avoid becoming another animal's lunch!

Unlike most butterfly species, buckeye butterflies, like this one, lay eggs on a variety of host plants.

Some butterflies have glands that release a fluid that makes predators think twice about making them a meal.

The eyespots on a buckeye butterfly are used to scare away predators.

Chasing Butterflies

· · · · · · · · · · · · · · · · · · · ·

I've been chasing butterflies
over field and farm.
I've been chasing butterflies,
wishing them no harm.

I've been chasing butterflies
with my little net.
I've been chasing butterflies,
but have not caught one yet.

I finally caught a butterfly.
Beauty in my net.
I held her ever so gently.
Studied her so intently.

She never stopped opening her wings.
It is a very good thing.
I could not keep my butterfly.
She looks better flying in the sky.

A Butterfly's Best Friend

A lepidopterist is a
person who studies or collects
butterflies and moths. People who
study lepidopterology have helped us learn
more about metamorphosis, different species of
butterflies, and all of the other important things we
now know and are still learning about butterflies!

Many butterflies, like this crimson-patched longwing, are named because of the colors or the designs on their wings.

Butterflies have compound eyes, which are eyes that are made up of thousands of tiny lenses.

Butterflies don't usually live for very long. Some can survive for months, whereas others only live a couple of weeks or days.

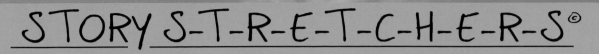

STORY S-T-R-E-T-C-H-E-R-S©

Stretch out the learning with this collection of activities created specifically to enhance the material and provide new ways to discover the wonderful world of butterflies. From language, to science, to art, to music, each activity incorporates information from the book and provides a new approach to teaching early learners in and out of the classroom. For more Story S-t-r-e-t-c-h-e-r-s©, please visit www.FlowerpotPress.com.

Story S-t-r-e-t-c-h-e-r© for SCIENCE

What the children will learn
To be keen observers of the markings on butterfly wings

Materials
Photographs of various butterflies, including a buckeye butterfly

What to do
1. Choose three different butterflies to compare. Be sure one of the three butterflies chosen is a buckeye butterfly.
2. Read the poem "I Spy," and let children guess which butterfly the poem is about.
3. Inform the children that it is the buckeye butterfly.
4. Teach the children to play the game "I Spy" by saying the phrase, "I spy with my little eye" and then name a characteristic of one of the butterflies in the photos.
5. After practicing the "I Spy" game with three butterfly photographs from above, add more photos for the children to use.

Something to think about
If possible, use real butterflies for the game. High-quality photographs also work, but watching real butterflies will help make the activity more interactive and engaging.

Story S-t-r-e-t-c-h-e-r© for LANGUAGE

What the children will learn
To learn the word "metamorphosis" and understand the concept as it relates to butterflies

Materials
Index cards; markers; and a chart tablet or whiteboard

What to do
1. Write the poem "Meta-Meta-Metamorphosis" on a whiteboard or chart tablet. Write the word "metamorphosis" and the last two lines of the poem in a different color.
2. Read the poem aloud to the children. Then read it a second time, and encourage the children to read along with you.
3. Ask the class to write the word "metamorphosis" on an index card and ask them what they think the word means based on the poem.
4. Together discuss the concept of metamorphosis. First define it, and then discuss how it applies to butterflies.

Something to think about
Try using this Story S-t-r-e-t-c-h-e-r with "Butterfly Big Words." It is another great poem to teach complex words and butterfly concepts.

Story S-t-r-e-t-c-h-e-r© for SCIENCE/LANGUAGE

What the children will learn
To observe the life cycle of a monarch butterfly and match the terminology to each step in the cycle

Materials
Monarch butterfly kits

What to do
1. Prepare children for the experience of the kits by discussing the stages of the life cycle of the butterfly.
2. Read the poems "Larva or Caterpillar" and "Caterpillar No More" to learn more about the butterfly life cycle.
3. When the kits arrive, follow the directions from the sources carefully. Note that some kits start with eggs on leaves, while others begin with the larva or caterpillars.
4. Carefully observe the chrysalis or pupa stage. Let the children mark off the dates on a calendar from the time they receive the kit to the end of the cycle when a butterfly emerges.

Something to think about
If you would prefer not to use a kit and you have a specific butterfly's host plant nearby, you can easily observe a butterfly's life cycle in their natural environment.

Story S-t-r-e-t-c-h-e-r© for MUSIC/MOVEMENT

What the children will learn
To sing a new song to a traditional tune

Materials
Chart tablet or whiteboard and markers

What to do
1. Print the words to the first stanza of "Here We Go Round the Mulberry Bush" on the chart tablet or whiteboard.
2. Teach the children to sing the traditional song "Here We Go Round the Mulberry Bush."
3. Next, write the words to the "Here We Go Round the Butterfly Bush" poem on the chart tablet or whiteboard.
4. Read the "Here We Go Round the Butterfly Bush" poem and substitute "butterfly bush" for "mulberry bush."
5. For older children, sing the entire poem to the tune of the traditional song and add the dramatics of the actions by dancing around a pretend butterfly bush.

Something to think about
To get the most out of this poem, visit an actual butterfly garden in the neighborhood or at a nature center.

Story S-t-r-e-t-c-h-e-r© for ART

What the children will learn
To create an art project using a swallowtail as inspiration

Materials
Swallowtail butterfly photographs; thick white art paper; scissors; thin strips of black construction paper; yellow, black, white, and blue tempura paints; small paint brushes; and cotton swabs

Optional materials: glitter glue or clear glue; short pencils or wooden sticks; and pipe cleaners

What to do
1. Read the "Swallowtails" poem.
2. Help the children recall some of the characteristics of swallowtails, specifically their pointy tails.
3. Show the children a variety of swallowtail photographs as examples, and then let them draw their own swallowtail shapes.
4. Once they have drawn the shape of their swallowtail, have them match their butterfly to one of the common types of swallowtails listed in the poem.
5. When they have decided which butterfly their drawing most closely resembles, ask them to draw the patterns and use the colors that best fit that specific swallowtail in their art.
6. After they complete their butterflies, allow them to dry overnight.
7. The next day, cut out the butterflies and display them around the room.

Something to think about
To make the butterflies multi-dimensional, add short pencils or wooden sticks for the thorax, twist pipe cleaners for the legs and antennae, glue on a black circle for the head, a tiny black dot for the compound eye, and use a slender black strip of paper for the proboscis.

GLOSSARY

Abdomen: the soft lower part of a butterfly's body

Adult: the fourth and final stage of a butterfly's life cycle

Antennae: rod-shaped body parts found on a butterfly's head; used to smell and maintain balance

Butterfly: a brightly colored flying insect

Caterpillar: the wormlike larva of a butterfly; the second stage of a butterfly's life cycle

Chitin: the protein that makes up a butterfly's wings

Chrysalis: the hard shell that covers the pupa

Compound Eye: a butterfly's eye which is made up of thousands of lens

Egg: the first stage of a butterfly's life cycle

Exoskeleton: the external covering of a butterfly

Host Plant: the home for a caterpillar; where butterflies will typically lay their eggs

Instar: the stages of a caterpillar between molts

Larva: the second stage of a butterfly's life cycle; another name for a caterpillar

Lepidopterist: a person who studies or collects butterflies

Life cycle: the series of changes a butterfly undergoes; there are four stages in a butterfly's life cycle

Metamorphosis: the transformation a butterfly goes through beginning as an egg and eventually becoming an adult

Migrate: to travel from one place to another like a monarch butterfly

Molt: when caterpillars shed their skin as they grow

Nectar: a sweet liquid that comes from plants; what many butterflies like to eat

Proboscis: the body part of a butterfly that is used for drinking

Prolegs: the false legs attached to the abdomen of a caterpillar

Pupa: the third stage of a butterfly's life cycle; it is also called a chrysalis

Thorax: the front part of a butterfly's body